Fudge Won't Lunge

Riddhi Maniar Doda

Illustrated by

Shivani J

Published by Scholastic India Pvt. Ltd.
A subsidiary of Scholastic Inc., New York, 10012 (USA).
Publishers since 1920, with international operations in Canada, Australia, New Zealand, the United Kingdom, India, and Hong Kong.

For information regarding permission, write to:
Scholastic India Pvt. Ltd.
A-27, Ground Floor, Sigma Centre
Infocity-1, Sector 34, Gurgaon-122001 (India)

First edition: April 2026

ISBN-13: 978-93-5954-614-8

Printed in India at : VK Global Digital Private Limited

Brown like chocolate and white like cream,

My dog Fudge is sweet or so it may seem.

It's just him and me at home today.

DinG! The doorbell rings as we start to play.

When I go to open the door,

Fudge suddenly runs out to explore!

Oh NO! I follow him quickly.
But he races ahead boldly.

Too fast for my tiny feet,
He enters a crowded street.

I say, 'Fudge, STOP'

But he jumps into a muddy puddle. PLOP!

I shout, 'Fudge, NOO!'

But he topples baskets of MANGO!

I command, 'Fudge, **Sit!**'
But does he listen?
Not even a bit!

Fed up, I scream,
'Fudge, **DOWN!**'

downnn

And he does! He lies down,
On the busiest street in town!

Surprised, I say, 'Fudge, **COME!**'
But now he doesn't – what a problem!

I push him gently to the left, and to the right,

I try to shove him using all my might.

I do all I can to lift his bottom, too.

But Fudge stays stuck like glue!

I look around helplessly.

Could somebody please help me?

A fish seller comes ahead.

She dangles a fish over Fudge's head.

Fudge twitches his **NOSE**.

But continues to doze.

A garland seller walks by.

He sprinkles water over Fudge's eye!

Fudge blinks his **EYES**.

But refuses to rise.

A girl cycles around.

Ringing the bell with a loud sound.

tRiiiNG!

Fudge pricks up his EaR.

But pretends not to hear!

Soon, a few street dogs come to smell him,

Like he is a tin of creamy cream.

Fudge wags his **tail**.

But still stays stuck like a snail.

Autorickshaws brake and turn

SCREECH

Passersby don't find this fun.

But Fudge does not seem to care.

He relaxes like a lion in his lair.

OW!

SHOO!

'Fudge, why don't you budge?'

I ask him with a grudge.

I give up and sit
outside a café,

Wondering what my
parents will say.

Just then, I see
something great.

Idea! All I need to
do is get...

Café Beagle
OPEN

The fishing rod
from the fish seller.

A bit of thread from
the garland seller.

Some help from the girl on the cycle.

And something special from Café Beagle!

Sniff Sniff!

Lick Lick!

One step, two steps, three,
four, and five.

Fudge gets up and

at home,
we arrive!

It takes a very fruity and very creamy piece of fudge,

To make my sweet little

FUDGE finally **BUDGE**!

Riddhi Maniar Doda stitches together themes of belonging, playfulness, and the quiet magic of everyday discovery in children's stories. Her tales draw upon the vibrant threads of contemporary Indian culture, bringing colourful characters and familiar worlds to life. Her other books for children include *The Boy Who Wore Bangles* and *Manvinder's Medu Vada.*

Shivani J is an illustrator and visual storyteller who loves creating dreamy, stylized, and colourful worlds. She finds inspiration in everything around her—small moments, emotions, places, and everyday life. When she's not drawing, you'll usually find her watching movies or playing games, quietly wandering and gathering inspiration along the way.